The No-BS Guide to ENDING BURNOUT & Reclaiming Your Power

Liz Atherton

CONSCIOUS CARE PUBLISHING PTY LTD

REKINDLING ME WORKBOOK
The No-BS Guide to Ending Burnout & Reclaiming Your Power

Copyright © 2025 by Liz Atherton. All rights reserved.

First Published 2025 by: Conscious Care Publishing Pty Ltd
www.consciouscarepublishing.com

First Edition printed November 2025.

Notice of Rights:

This book is sold subject to the condition that it shall not, by way of trade or otherwise, be lent, resold, hired out, or otherwise circulated without the publisher's prior consent, in any form of binding or cover, other than that in which it is published, and without a similar condition, including this condition being imposed on the subsequent purchaser. All rights reserved by the publisher. No part of this publication may be reproduced, stored in a retrieval system, or transmitted in any form, or by any means, electronic, digital, mechanical, photocopying, scanning, recorded or otherwise, without the prior written permission of the copyright owner. Requests to the copyright owner should be addressed to Permissions Department, Conscious Care Publishing Pty Ltd, PO Box 2399, Redcliffe North, QLD 4020, Australia, email: admin@consciouscare.com

Limits of Liability/Disclaimer of Warranty:

The practices, perspectives, and tools in this book are offered for educational and personal development purposes only. They are not intended as a substitute for psychological, medical, or psychiatric treatment or professional advice. While the author has over 25 years of experience as a life coach, intuitive guide, and spiritual mentor, the author is not a licensed psychologist, therapist, or medical professional. The guidance within this book is drawn from client work, intuitive insight, my own healing journey, and teachings received through spirit and Higher Self connection. Every reader is responsible for how they engage with and apply the material in this book. If you are experiencing significant emotional distress or mental health challenges, please seek the support of a qualified professional. This book is not meant to diagnose, treat, or cure any condition. What you choose to do with the information here is entirely your responsibility, and your healing journey is sacred, personal, and always your own.

While the publisher and author have used their best efforts in preparing this book, they make no representations or warranties with respect to the accuracy or completeness of the contents of this book and specifically disclaim any implied warranties of merchantability or fitness for a particular purpose. No warranty may be created or extended by sales representatives or written sales materials. The advice and strategies contained herein may not be suitable for your situation. You should consult with a professional where appropriate. The intent of the author is only to offer information for a general nature. Neither the publisher nor author shall be liable for any loss of profit or any other commercial damages, including but not limited to special, incidental, consequential, or other damages. The author and the publisher assume no responsibility for your actions.

Where photographic images have been provided by the author and people are depicted, such images are being used for illustrative purposes only. Product names may be trademarks or registered trademarks, and are used for identification and explanation without intent to infringe. Conscious Care Publishing publishes in a variety of print and electronic format and by print-on-demand. Some material included with standard print versions of this book may not be included in e-books or in print-on-demand. If this book refers to media such as a downloadable, CD or DVD that is not included in the version you purchased, you may download this material at the website nominated in the "Next Steps" section of this book.

National Library of Australia Cataloguing-in-Publication entry:
Author: Atherton, Liz
Rekindling Me / By Liz Atherton

ISBN 9780645089288 (Paperback)
ISBN 9780645089295 (ePub)
ISBN 9780987633729 (Workbook)
ISBN 9780987633736 (Audiobook)
ISBN 9781764210409 (Hardback)

Printed by Lightning Source
Typeset & cover design by Conscious Care Publishing Pty Ltd
ISBN: 978-0-9876337-2-9

CONTENTS

CHAPTER 1 - THE EXHAUSTION OF BEING THE STRONG ONE	1
CHAPTER 2 - BORN TO BELONG, TAUGHT TO TRADE: THE HIDDEN CURRENCY OF CHILDHOOD	4
CHAPTER 3 - YOU'RE NOT BROKEN – YOU'RE RUNNING OUTDATED SOFTWARE	7
CHAPTER 4 - THE ARCHITECTURE OF STRESS: UNDERSTANDING THE INNER VOICES OF THE MIND	12
CHAPTER 5 - STRESS ISN'T THE PROBLEM – IT'S THE MESSAGE	17
CHAPTER 6 - HOW YOUR NERVOUS SYSTEM SHAPES YOUR INNER DIALOGUE	20
CHAPTER 7 - DECODING EMOTIONAL TRIGGERS: PATHWAYS TO HEALING	30
CHAPTER 8 - WHEN THE PAST SPEAKS THROUGH YOU: WHY OLD PROGRAMS DISTORT VOICE, TONE, AND PRESENCE	35
CHAPTER 9 - WHY MINDSET ALONE CAN'T CLEAR TRIGGERS	40
CHAPTER 10 - WHAT REWIRES THESE PATTERNS – SCIENCE + SOUL	43
CHAPTER 11 - BUILDING EMOTIONAL SAFETY WITHIN	45
CHAPTER 12 - THE LANGUAGE OF THE HIGHER SELF	47
CHAPTER 13 - CONSCIOUS BOUNDARIES AND SOUL INTEGRITY	51
CHAPTER 14 - RECLAIMING YOUR AUTHENTIC VOICE	55
CHAPTER 15 - INTEGRATING THE ARCHITECTURE: LIVING THE SHIFT	59

	NATURAL EMOTIONS	DISTORTED EMOTIONS
FEAR	Fight/Flight/Freeze impulse, cautious, startled	Greed, obstinate, suspicious, overcautious, frightened, worry, anxious, petrified, panicked and phobias
LOVE	Blissful, self-confident, giving and receiving, kindness, nurturing, emotional support and self-love	Controlling, demanding, possessive, abandoned, and dominating, inadequate, insecure, instability of love.
ANGER	Used to bring about change, self protects, assertive and firm with self and others	Rage, hatred, frustrated, bitterness, self-hate, resentment, aggressive, hurt, powerless, no inner authority, defeated, cheated and intimidated.
JEALOUS	Impels and motivates us to grow, improve our self worth, model from another person's behaviour	Envious, deceitful, criticism of self and others, competitive and comparative
GRIEF	Sharing of feelings, loss and tears	Depression, blame, regret, remorse, guilty, self-pity, martyrdom or suicidal

1

THE EXHAUSTION OF BEING THE STRONG ONE

Before we go deeper into how these patterns form, take a moment to look honestly at your own experience. You may recognise yourself in some of the patterns we just explored. See what resonates with you.

Ask yourself:

- Do I feel responsible for holding things together for others?

- Do people come to me when they need help, advice, or emotional support?

THE EXHAUSTION OF BEING THE STRONG ONE

- Do I find it difficult to ask for help, or do I rarely even think to ask, even when I need it?

- Do I keep going when I am exhausted because others rely on me?

- Do I feel resentful when my efforts go unnoticed?

- Do I struggle to relax when things feel out of control around me?

- Do I often feel like the strong one in my family, relationships, or workplace?

If several of these resonate, you may have learned early in life that strength and usefulness were the safest ways to stay connected to others.

There is nothing wrong with being capable or dependable. But when strength becomes the only role you feel allowed to play, it can quietly disconnect you from your own needs.

Now ask yourself something deeper:

- Where did I first learn that I needed to be the strong one?
- Was it in my family?
- In my relationships?
- In moments where I felt I had no other choice?

Take a few minutes to write whatever comes to mind. There is no right or wrong answer here. The goal is simply awareness.

Because once you begin to see the pattern, you are already one step closer to changing it.

BORN TO BELONG, TAUGHT TO TRADE: THE HIDDEN CURRENCY OF CHILDHOOD

Reflection Prompt

Take a quiet moment to reflect on this question:

- Where in my life am I trading my time, energy, truth, or peace in exchange for love, approval, or safety?

Now ask yourself the deeper question:

- What am I most afraid to lose, and how often do I abandon myself to keep it?

There is no need for shame. This is simply about awareness. Naming the trade is the first act of reclaiming your power.

Simple Exercise

For the next 3 days, choose one interaction per day; at work, in family, in friendship or partnership, and reflect:

- What did I give?
- What did I hope to receive in return?
- Was this trade aligned with my truth, or driven by fear?
- If I had traded consciously, what would I have done differently?

Write it down. Don't edit yourself. Let the truth rise.

Day 1:

Day 2:

Day 3:

By the end of the three days, look at your notes and ask:

What patterns do I see?

What's one trade am I ready to stop making?

That one choice could be the beginning of returning to your true self.

3

YOU'RE NOT BROKEN – YOU'RE RUNNING OUTDATED SOFTWARE

Reflection Prompt

Where do I still trade parts of myself for love, safety, or approval?

```
┌─────────────────────────────────────────────────────────┐
│                                                         │
│                                                         │
│                                                         │
│                                                         │
│                                                         │
└─────────────────────────────────────────────────────────┘
```

What would it feel like to live from my core, without the fear of rejection?

```
┌─────────────────────────────────────────────────────────┐
│                                                         │
│                                                         │
│                                                         │
│                                                         │
│                                                         │
└─────────────────────────────────────────────────────────┘
```

Journal Exercise – Writing to Your Inner Child

Write a letter to the part of you that felt unsupported or abandoned.

Let them know you are here now that they are no longer alone. That their needs matter, their pain is valid, and they don't have to carry it anymore.

Offer them compassion, and begin to rebuild the bridge between your Adult Self and the Inner Child within.

Belief Rewriting Practice

List three outdated beliefs from childhood.

Then, for each one, write a new belief that reflects your truth today.

Example:
- **Old:** *"My needs are a burden."*
- **New:** *"My needs are valid and deserve to be met."*

1. Old Belief

1. New Belief

2. Old Belief

2. New Belief

3. Old Belief

3. New Belief

4

THE ARCHITECTURE OF STRESS: UNDERSTANDING THE INNER VOICES OF THE MIND

Reflection Prompt - "Who's Speaking for Me?"

As you move through daily conversations, begin asking:

"Who is speaking for me right now?"

- Is it the wounded Inner Child seeking safety or validation?
- Is it the critical Inner Parent enforcing shame or control?
- Is it the Adult Self trying to manage the moment, keep peace, or fix?
- Or is it the Higher Self—clear, calm, grounded in truth?

 THE ARCHITECTURE OF STRESS

Journal Prompt - Mapping My Voices

Choose a recent emotionally charged moment or conversation.

Now reflect and write:

1. What happened?

2. What did I feel in my body?

3. What thoughts or inner dialogue came up?

4. Which voice do I believe was most active?

5. Which voice was missing?

6. What might my Higher Self have said or done differently?

Realignment Practice - Rewriting the Inner Dialogue

Take a moment to write compassionate replies from your Adult Self and Higher Self to any dominant Inner Child or Inner Parent beliefs you noticed.

Example:

- Inner Child: *"I'm not safe to speak up."*
- Adult Self: *"That fear makes sense—but we're safe now."*
- Higher Self: *"Your voice matters. You're safe to speak truth with love."*

Awareness Integration - End-of-Day Voice Check-In

Each evening, ask yourself:

1. Who led my conversations today—fear, control, or compassion?

```
[                                                                    ]
```

2. How did I feel before, during, and after key interactions?

```
[                                                                    ]
```

3. What intention can I carry forward tomorrow to invite my Higher Self to guide my voice more often?

```
[                                                                    ]
```

Inviting the Higher Self to Lead My Voice (Daily Reflection)

Find a quiet space. Sit comfortably. Allow your hands to rest softly. Close your eyes if you wish. Begin to breathe gently, slowly, and entirely—in through the nose, out through the mouth.

With each breath, allow your body to settle…
… softening the shoulders…
… releasing the jaw…
… grounding your feet.

Now bring to mind the conversation you are preparing for. See the person (or people) you will be speaking with. Feel the energy of this interaction in your body—without judgment, just noticing.

Now, gently ask yourself:

1. **Pause. Breathe** deeply.

2. **Ask:** "Who do I want to speak for me in this moment? My fear, my wounded Inner Child, my inner critic…or the wise, compassionate voice of my Higher Self?"

3. **Hand on heart. Breathe again. Say:** "I call on the deepest truth within me—the part of me that sees with love, speaks with clarity, and honours both self and other."

4. **Intention:** "Let my words today be shaped not by fear, but by compassion. Let me listen with curiosity. Let me speak with kindness. Let me remember that we are both whole beings, doing our best."

5. **Pause. Breathe.** Feel this alignment settling in your body.

6. **Breathe.** Begin your conversation with presence.

7. When you are ready, open your eyes, carrying this awareness into your conversation.

5

STRESS ISN'T THE PROBLEM – IT'S THE MESSAGE

Self-Reconnection Practice:

Take a moment to check in with yourself. Inner conflict often whispers in your reactions, your stress, and your sense of disconnection. But it can also become the gateway to your most significant transformation.

Reflect on the following questions in your journal or quiet time:

1. Which of my emotional reactions feel "justified" but still leave me disempowered? What belief might be driving those reactions?

````



````

2. Where in my life am I currently experiencing the most inner conflict?

````



````

3. Are the emotions I feel in these situations natural (present, grounded) or distorted (fear-based, reactive)?

4. Can I trace these reactions back to earlier beliefs or childhood conditioning?

5. What version of me do I become when I'm trying to stay safe or earn love?

6. What would my life look like if I trusted natural emotions as my compass instead of letting distorted emotions steer?

Realignment Practice:

The next time you're emotionally triggered, pause. Ask: *"Is this a natural emotion responding to the present, or a distorted emotion reacting to the past?"* Journal your answer. Observe without judgment.

This week, choose one recurring emotional reaction, something that regularly makes you feel powerless, angry, anxious, or unseen. Each time it surfaces, pause and ask:

"Is this emotion a reflection of my present truth? Or a memory from my past?"

Breathe. Give the emotion space to exist without judgment. Then gently invite a more natural emotion into the space. This is not about forcing joy. It's about choosing alignment, one honest shift at a time.

6

HOW YOUR NERVOUS SYSTEM SHAPES YOUR INNER DIALOGUE

Reflection Prompts for Speaking from a Regulated State

1. **Listening to My Body First**

   Daily Check-In

   - When did my body speak before my mind today?
   - What signs of stress or safety did I notice in my breath, posture, or tone?
   - How did that influence the way I communicated?

   Alignment Intention: I commit to noticing: *"Where is this response starting? In my body or my mind?"*

ReKindling Me   HOW THE NERVOUS SYSTEM SHAPES

2. **Mapping My Mind-Body Connection**

   Evening Reflection

   - When did my body feel stressed before I consciously knew why?
   - When did a thought or worry create tension in my body?
   - How did either shape the tone, words, or energy in my communication?

   Alignment Intention: *I will begin tracking how my body and mind interact, so I can shift with awareness.*

ReKindling Me

3. **Spotting My State in the Moment**

   Mini Pause Practice (2–3x/day)

   - What state am I in right now?

     (Safe → calm / Fight-flight → tense / Freeze → shut down)

   - What are the clues?

     (My breath? My tone? My body language?)

   - How is this affecting what I say? Or don't say?

   Alignment Intention: *I pause, name my state, and invite presence before I speak.*

4. **Listening to My Inner Voice**

   In Moments of Emotional Charge

   - What is the voice in my head saying right now?
   - Is it calm, fearful, critical, or supportive?
   - Is this my Higher Self, or a protective part?

   Alignment Intention: *I notice the voice and choose whether to follow it.*

5. **Who Was Speaking for Me Today?**

   End-of-Day Check-In

   - In a key interaction, what state was I in (calm, anxious, shut down)?
   - Who was leading? Inner Child, Inner Parent, Adult Self or Higher Self?
   - What helped me notice this? (Tone, thoughts, breath?)
   - What could I try next time to shift faster into alignment?

   Alignment Intention: *I reflect without judgment, and choose more consciously next time.*

6. **Am I Speaking from Distortion or Clarity?**

   Before a Conversation

   - What emotion am I bringing in?
   - Is this a natural, present-moment emotion, or a distortion from an old belief?
   - How might this shape my tone, expression, or presence?

   Alignment Intention: *I pause and ask: "Is this my truth? Or my old survival strategy?"*

7. **How Is My Body Speaking Through My Voice?**

   After a Conversation or a Trigger

   - How did my tone, pace, or presence feel?
   - Did I speak from calm or anxiety, shutdown, or people-pleasing?
   - What felt aligned and what didn't?

   Alignment Intention: *I use my voice as a mirror and adjust with self-compassion.*

8. **How Am I Supporting My Change?**

   Self-Support Check-In

   - What practices (breathwork, grounding, movement) help me stay calm?
   - Where could I use more support (e.g., somatic work, belief clearing, facilitation)?
   - What would it feel like to allow myself to be helped truly?

   Alignment Intention: *I deserve support. I allow myself what helps me grow.*

9. **Choosing My Tools for Change**

   Empowered Planning

   - What tools have helped me shift my voice, triggers, or stress response?
   - Which ones could I deepen or return to now?
   - Where could I ask for guidance or co-regulation?

   Alignment Intention: *I utilise every tool available to help me reconnect with my true self.*

10. Which Voice Is Leading Me?

Real-Time Awareness Practice

- What state is my body in right now?
- Who is speaking? Inner Child, Inner Parent, Adult Self, or Higher Self?
- Am I responding from love, fear, or habit?

Alignment Intention: *I choose my speaker with care, presence, and truth.*

11. Preparing My Voice for Change

Voice Repatterning Reflection

- What beliefs are still shaping my tone or presence?
- Where am I ready to let go of survival-based patterns?
- What simple practice can help me stay regulated and congruent today?

Alignment Intention: *My voice is allowed to reflect the truth I now live.*

12. What's This Emotion Telling Me?

Trigger Inquiry Practice

- Is this a natural, clear emotion, or a distorted emotion from the past?
- What belief, memory, or expectation is this emotion referencing?
- What would my Higher Self want me to know right now?

13. Journal Prompt - Emotional Pattern Mapping

Think of one emotional reaction this week that surprised or overwhelmed you.

Write:

- What happened?
- What did I feel in my body?
- What belief was driving this?
- What would a natural response have looked like?
- What truth is my Higher Self inviting me into?

14. Realignment Practice - Distorted vs. Natural Emotion

Choose one recurring emotional pattern (e.g., anxiety, anger, avoidance). For 3 days:

Each time it surfaces, pause and ask:

- *"Is this from now or from the past?"*
- *"What belief or fear is being triggered?"*
- *"What new truth could I try instead?"*

Alignment Intention: One pause. One breath. One realignment at a time.

7

DECODING EMOTIONAL TRIGGERS: PATHWAYS TO HEALING

Becoming conscious of your triggers doesn't start with changing how you feel. It starts with observing when and where the emotional charge takes over. This is the practice of self-awareness in real time: not to shame or fix, but to learn, soften, and rewire.

Below are guided prompts and practices to help you begin recognising where your past may be shaping your present, especially in your communication.

Awareness Practice: "Where Did I React from a Layer?"

At the end of the day or week, reflect on your interactions:

- Where did I overreact to something small?
- Where did I shut down, retreat, or become defensive without fully understanding why?
- Was my response actually about the current person or moment… or was it about something deeper inside me?

Use this guiding sentence:

"I wasn't reacting to the person in front of me. I was reacting to the layer of _____ inside me."

Examples:

- *"…the rejection I felt in childhood."*
- *"…my belief that I'm not good enough."*
- *"…my fear that I'll be abandoned."*

Let the insight come without judgment. You're not wrong for reacting. You're just meeting yourself more clearly now.

Real-Time Trigger Spotting Exercise

In your next few conversations, especially the emotionally charged or uncomfortable ones:

1. **Pause for 3 to 5 seconds before speaking.**
   - This gives your nervous system a moment to stabilise.
   - Ask silently: *"Is this my true voice, or a reaction from the past?"*

2. **Observe your body:**
   - Is there heat, tightness, clenching, or shallow breathing?
   - Is your tone sharper, louder, flatter, or overly sweet?

3. **Spot the voice:**
   - Is this my Inner Child trying to be heard?
   - Is this my Inner Parent trying to control?
   - Is my Adult Self or Higher Self online right now?

4. **Optional reframe (silently or aloud):**
   - *"What I really need right now is…"*
   - *"I'm feeling something deeper than just this moment."*
   - *"Let me pause. I want to respond with more clarity."*

Journal Reflection Prompts:

Use these as daily or weekly journaling anchors:

- What conversation challenged me most this week?
- What part of me was leading that conversation? Inner Child, Inner Parent, Adult Self?
- What emotional or physical signs told me I was triggered?
- What was I *really* afraid of in that moment?
- What would my Higher Self have said or done differently?

Alignment Intention:

"I commit to recognising when the past is speaking through me and choosing presence instead of pattern."

You may not catch every trigger in the moment, and that's okay. Every time you reflect on an experience after the fact, you build your capacity to respond differently next time. That is healing. That is rewiring.

8

WHEN THE PAST SPEAKS THROUGH YOU: WHY OLD PROGRAMS DISTORT VOICE, TONE, AND PRESENCE

Reflection Prompt - "Who Spoke for Me?"

Think of a conversation this week where you walked away feeling off, regretful, or emotionally stirred.

Ask yourself:

- What did I say. How did I say it?
- Did my tone, volume, or body language reflect fear, pressure, or performance?
- Which belief might have been silently driving how I spoke?
- Was it my Higher Self, Inner Child, Inner Parent, or rational Adult Self speaking?

Trigger Trace Exercise - Belief to Voice Map

Complete this for one conversation where you felt your voice wasn't congruent like in the table below:

Situation	What I Said	How I Said it	What I Felt	Likely Subconscious Belief	What I Wish I'd Said Instead
Example: My partner questioned my plans	*"It's fine, I'll figure it out."*	Flat tone, quiet, looked away	Resentment, shutdown	*"I'm too much if I have needs."*	*"I do have a plan, and I'd love your support."*

Repeat for 1–2 recent conversations.

WHEN THE PAST SPEAKS THROUGH YOU

Somatic Check-In - Voice Awareness

Next time you speak, especially under pressure, pause and notice:

- What is my breath doing right now?
- How does my voice sound; fast, flat, tight, soft, hesitant?
- What does my body posture suggest I believe in this moment?

Then try this grounding alignment: Hand on heart. Breathe deep. Ask: *"Is this my survival voice or my true voice?"*

Alignment Intention - Shaping Your Voice from Truth

Choose a daily mantra for the week ahead. Let it become an anchor when your old voice starts to lead:

- *"I don't need to prove. I just need to speak from presence."*
- *"My tone matters more than my script."*
- *"My truth can be soft and still powerful."*
- *"I can speak with kindness, without shrinking or performing."*

Journal Prompt - Reclaiming My Real Voice

- What belief has most distorted my voice in the past?
- How did I learn to speak that way? Where did I pick it up?
- How would my voice sound if I were completely safe, calm, and aligned with truth?
- What would it feel like to speak with that voice today?

9

WHY MINDSET ALONE CAN'T CLEAR TRIGGERS

Reflection Practice: Noticing My Internal Battle

Take a moment to reflect on a time recently when you felt emotionally overwhelmed or reactive.

Ask yourself:

- Which part of me was leading? My Inner Child, Inner Parent, or Adult Self?
- What did I most need in that moment? Soothing, safety, boundaries, rest, compassion?
- What belief might have been driving my reaction?

Integration Practice: Voice Mapping My Patterns

Choose one common emotional pattern you notice in yourself (e.g. people-pleasing, shutting down, defensiveness).

- When does it usually appear?
- Which voice drives it? Inner Child, Inner Parent, Adult Self or Higher Self?
- What does it sound like in your tone, language, or presence?
- What might your Higher Self want you to remember when this pattern arises again?

Awareness Prompt

"I know better, but I still react..."

Gently explore a moment where this felt true for you. What does that part of you still believe it must do to stay safe? What might it need instead?

Realignment Intention

This week, I will notice when I'm reacting from past programming and pause to ask:

"Is this belief still true for who I am now?"
"Can I invite my Higher Self or Adult Self to lead instead?"

10

WHAT REWIRES THESE PATTERNS – SCIENCE + SOUL

Reflection Prompt: Where Am I Still Living from the Past?

Take a few moments to reflect on this question:

- In what area of my life do I still speak, act, or choose from an old pattern, not from who I am now?
- What belief, emotion, or reflex is still shaping my tone or presence in those moments?

Integration Inquiry: Feeling vs. Forcing the Change

Notice the difference between times when you've tried to think your way out of a pattern vs. when you've felt the shift in your body. Ask:

- What emotional charge still feels active in me?
- What part of me (Inner Child, Inner Parent) still needs to be heard, held, or updated?

Realignment Intention

This week, when I notice a reactive response rise in me, I will pause and ask:

- Has this pattern been cleared at the root or am I trying to manage it with effort alone?
- Can I invite my Higher Self to guide me through this, gently?

Higher Self Whisper

Close your eyes and breathe into your heart. Imagine your Higher Self placing a hand on your shoulder and saying:

- *"You are safe now. You don't need to protect yourself the same way anymore. I've got you."*

11

BUILDING EMOTIONAL SAFETY WITHIN

Reflection Prompt: Where Do I Still Outsource My Safety?

Take a few minutes to ask yourself gently:

- In what moments do I still wait for others to validate, soothe, or approve of me before I feel safe to speak, act, or rest?
- What part of me (Inner Child or Inner Parent) is trying to control or avoid those moments?

Integration Prompt: Rebuilding Trust with Myself

Ask yourself:

- What is one small way I could show myself today that I won't abandon my truth?
- What promise could I keep to myself that would rebuild trust, even a little?

Realignment Intention

This week, I will practise being my own safe home.

- I will listen to what I need.
- I will speak to myself with a kind, regulating tone.
- I will remind my nervous system: *"You are safe. I'm here with you."*

Higher Self Whisper

Imagine your Higher Self kneeling beside you and saying gently:

- *"You don't have to earn rest. You don't have to perform to be safe. You are allowed to be. I'm not going anywhere."*

12

THE LANGUAGE OF THE HIGHER SELF

Reflection & Integration: Tuning into the Language of Your Higher Self

Daily Awareness Prompt:

At the end of each day, take a moment to reflect:

- When did I feel most connected to calm, clear inner guidance today?
- What did that voice sound or feel like in my body?
- Did I follow it—or override it with fear, urgency, or doubt?

Journal Prompt – Meeting the Higher Self in Real Time:

Think back to a moment recently when you felt anxious, uncertain, or emotionally reactive.

- What voice was leading in that moment—Inner Child, Inner Parent, Adult Self or Higher Self?
- What did each part want to say?
- If the Higher Self had been leading, what might it have said instead?

Practice – Rewriting the Survival Voice:

Choose one recurring internal statement you often hear when stressed or afraid.

Examples:

- "I'm going to mess this up."
- "They're not going to accept me."
- "I have to fix this or else…"

Now, rewrite this statement through the voice of your Higher Self.

Examples:

- "Even if I don't get this perfect, I can handle the outcome with grace."
- "I am not for everyone—and that's okay."
- "I can face this moment with clarity and trust myself."

Repeat your Higher Self reframe out loud—gently, calmly, and with grounded presence.

Self-Awareness Check-In:

Pause throughout the day and ask:

- *"What part of me is speaking right now—my fear, my past, or my Higher Self?"*
- *"What would truth say in this moment?"*

Let that voice guide your next action or response.

Higher Self Connection Practice:

Each morning or evening, take 2–3 minutes to breathe deeply and ask inwardly:

- *"Higher Self, what do I need to hear today?"*
- Write down the first calm, clear message you sense or feel, without forcing.

This is how the relationship strengthens: not through perfection, but through presence.

Alignment Intention:

I will create more quiet moments in my day so that I can hear, feel, and follow the calm, guiding voice of my Higher Self.

13

CONSCIOUS BOUNDARIES AND SOUL INTEGRITY

Journal Reflection – Listening to My Boundary Voice

Take a quiet moment and reflect:

- When was the last time I said *"Yes"* when I really meant *"No"*?
- What part of me was speaking in that moment—my Inner Child, Inner Parent, Adult Self or Higher Self?
- What did I fear would happen if I honoured my truth?
- What would my Higher Self have said or done instead?

CONSCIOUS BOUNDARIES AND SOUL INTEGRITY

Integration Prompt - Rewriting My Boundary Script

Think of a boundary you've been afraid to set.

Write out how you've been avoiding it—what words you've used (or haven't used).

Now rewrite it from the voice of your Higher Self.

Maintain a calm, grounded, and clear tone.

Example:

    Old version: *"I don't know... I guess I can help again."*

    Higher Self version: *"I care about you, and I'm not available for that right now. I need to protect my energy."*

CONSCIOUS BOUNDARIES AND SOUL INTEGRITY

Awareness Practice – Noticing My Boundary Reflexes

Over the next 3 days, notice how you respond in situations where your needs, time, or truth are being tested.

Ask yourself in real time:

- Am I speaking from fear, habit, or alignment?
- What am I afraid will happen if I say no or speak honestly?
- What emotion is rising in my body when I think about setting a boundary—guilt, fear, panic, shame?
- What does my nervous system need right now to feel safe enough to speak truthfully?

Higher Self Check-In – Before the Boundary Conversation

Before a challenging conversation or moment where you'll need to honour a boundary, pause and ask:

- *"What does truth sound like here?"*
- *"What does love sound like toward me and others?"*
- *"What does my Inner Child need to feel safe—and how can I protect that without collapsing?"*

Then breathe, slow down, and speak from that grounded place.

Realignment Reminder – After a Difficult Boundary

If someone reacts poorly to your boundary, take a moment to realign inwardly. Say to yourself:

- *"Their discomfort doesn't mean I was wrong."*
- *"My job is to stay in integrity—not to manage their emotional process."*
- *"I can be kind and still say no."*

Write down how you feel after standing in your truth. Let yourself notice the difference between guilt and growth.

Ongoing Intention – Anchoring Soul-Led Boundaries

Set this intention and revisit it daily for one week:

> *"I will speak from my centre, not from fear. I will let my boundaries reflect who I truly am, not who I've been trained to be."*

14

RECLAIMING YOUR AUTHENTIC VOICE

Journal Reflection – When Did I Stop Speaking Freely?

Take a quiet moment to reflect:

- Can I recall a time when I silenced my voice to stay safe, be liked, or avoid conflict?
- What did I fear would happen if I had spoken my truth?
- What belief did I form in that moment about using my voice?
- Is that belief still running my communication today?

 RECLAIMING YOUR AUTHENTIC VOICE

Daily Practice - Checking Who's Speaking

For the next three days, pause at least once during any key conversation and ask:

- What part of me is speaking? Inner Child, Inner Parent, Adult Self, or Higher Self?
- Am I speaking from performance, protection, or presence?
- How does my body feel as I speak? Tight, soft, braced, grounded?

Voice Reframe Prompt - From Distortion to Truth

Choose one phrase or tone you often use that feels distorted or inauthentic.

For example:

"Sorry, I just thought..."

Now rewrite it from your authentic voice:

"Here's something I'd like to share."

Repeat this reframe aloud. Let it land in your body. Practice it during your day.

Grounding Practice – Speak After the Breath

Before speaking in emotionally charged moments, practise this micro-pause:

- Inhale slowly. Exhale fully.
- Feel your feet on the floor.
- Ask yourself: *"What does my Higher Self want to say?"*

Let that voice, not your survival reflex, guide your next words.

Integration Prompt – My Voice in Leadership

Ask yourself:

- Where in my life am I still dimming or distorting my voice to be accepted or avoid discomfort?
- What would change in my relationships, leadership, or self-worth if I let my true voice lead, even softly?
- What fear comes up when I imagine being fully seen and heard?
- What does my Higher Self want me to know about that fear?

Intention Anchor – Voice as Soul

Set this intention today and repeat it often:

"My voice is sacred. I don't need to shout or shrink. I need to speak from my truth."

Reminder Phrase – When It Feels Scary to Be Heard

- *"My voice is not a threat, it's a truth."*
- *"If I speak with presence, I am safe, even in discomfort."*
- *"What truth wants is to be spoken, even if my voice shakes."*

15

INTEGRATING THE ARCHITECTURE: LIVING THE SHIFT

Reflection Prompt - Integration Awareness

Ask yourself:

- *"What's different in me now that can't be unseen?"*

Let this answer rise from within, not as a list, but as a knowing.

- What inner voice have I learned to hear more clearly? My Inner Child, Inner Parent, Adult Self, or Higher Self?
- In what ways do I now lead myself differently than before?
- Where am I no longer led by fear, but guided by truth?

Alignment Practice - Return to Presence

Today, pause during a moment of tension or decision-making and gently ask:

- Which part of me is speaking right now?
- What would my Higher Self choose in this moment?
- How can I honour both my humanity and my soul in how I respond?

Journal Reflection - Soul Integrity in Daily Life

Write freely on the following:

- Where in my life am I now choosing congruence over performance?
- When did I last feel proud of honouring my truth, even if it was hard?
- What am I no longer willing to sacrifice for approval or safety?

Final Realignment Prompt

Take a breath. Place your hand over your heart and ask:

- What does it mean for me to live the shift, not just understand it?
- What commitment do I now make, to my voice, my truth, and my soul-led path?

You've Finished Great Job!

www.ingramcontent.com/pod-product-compliance
Lightning Source LLC
Chambersburg PA
CBHW081420300426
44110CB00016BA/2334